The History of Bagels in America

By Marc Fintz

Fintz, Marc
The History of Bagels in America

39 pages

ISBN#: 978-1-79477-726-2

Inquiries or additional information contact:

All Natural Products,Inc
727 Drake Street
Bronx, NY 10474
Email: marc@allnp.com
www.allnp.cpm

Or visit

www.lulu.com

PRINTED IN THE UNITED STATES OF AMERICA

About the Author

Marc Fintz is a Business Development Officer, Consultant, and Food Historian speaking and writing about NYC's Artisan and Jewish Foods. He has authored a highly successful book called **The Rise and Fall of H&H Bagels**. He has appeared on such programs as Andrew Zimmern's *Bizarre Foods America*, and Food Insider's *History of the Babka*. He is the producer of the *Bagel Talk* YouTube series. He has worked with the famous Davidovich Bakery for the last 10 years.

This work is transcribed from a lecture series on the history of Jewish Foods, hosted by the Davidovich Bakery, on the Lower East Side of New York City in the Summer of 2019. The work is a transcription of the July 2019 lecture on the "The History of Bagels in America" by Marc Fintz, which took place at the historic Blue Moon Hotel before a sold out crowd. The text has not been changed from the spoken lecture in order to capture the essence of the lecture so it should be read in the mindset that it is a transcription and was not written originally for printed publication.

The Introduction

My name is Mark Fintz. Welcome to a special edition of *"Bagel Talk"*. I am here on the historic Lower East Side of New York City, at the Blue Moon Hotel, at the Davidovich Bagel Bakery location. Today we are going to be doing a talk on the history of bagels in America. We are right across from famous The Tenement Museum. We are in the historic place where bagels came to America for the first time from Polish immigrants in Eastern Europe. We are going to talk a little bit about the popularization of the product, what it means to be a real bagel, and about whether or not the bagel has moved from being simply a cultural and religious identifiable product to being a truly an American product. So, we're going to go inside and we'll get started with that. Thank you. (July 24, 2019 NYC)

The Lecture

I have been involved in the in the bagel business for the last twelve years. While I am not a bagel historian, it is a topic of great interest to me and I wrote a book, which was very well reviewed called: *__The Rise and Fall of H&H Bagels__*,[1] about the demise of one of the most famous bagel places in modern New York history.

So, I want to talk to you today a little bit about a subject that you may know a little bit about. To start out with let's look at these two products (holds up a kaiser Roll and a Davidovich plain bagel). They are all very familiar, you find them both in any deli pretty much in all of New York, and you find this product (holding up the Davidovich brand bagel) which is also a bagel, a plain bagel, namely a Davidovich Bagel. What's the difference between them? We will put taste aside and the subjective aspects of it aside and one might say: *"well, this is bread and this is a bagel"* but, it's more than that, because they're both basically bread products.

In my mind, the greatest distinction is that for people, particularly people in New York, most people don't have a story to tell about the kaiser roll, about their parents taking them to the kaiser roll

---

[1] Zirogiannis, Marc. **The Rise and Fall of H&H Bagels**. RWG Publishing Company. 2015.

store and getting that first egg sandwich on a kaiser roll, but the bagel is very different. It is a very different product, because more than just being food, and more than just being sustenance, it is tied into an identity.

Now, this product, (the Davidovich bagel) to some degree, is tied into an ethnic identity and a geographic identity and it becomes tied into a religious identity, becomes tied into a cultural identity, becomes tied into a city identity and, some might argue, today becomes part of the American identity and that's a little bit of what we're going to talk about.

So, historically, tracing the bagel's roots is a little bit hard for folks. We can go to the 14th century, before the 14th century there is not too much written about it. From the 14th to 16th century it is still a little gray; there's some notation of the bagels in 14th century writings. There are products that are very similar to the bagel, like the Taralli, coming out of Italy, a very similar product. There are some Polish products which are very very similar. Russian products, too, under different names, but any discussion of the product we recognize is referenced only in relationship to the Jewish Bakers of Eastern Europe. We don't really see the product being referred to as a bagel until the 16th century in Poland.

Now, as for the origins that pre-date the 16th Century it seems that from everything that I have read, that there is a very strong connection between the stadium pretzel and a bagel. They are very similar and, in fact, the original bagels, for reasons that we will talk about, were much similar in consistency to pretzels. They both have a thick outer crust and are both doughy on the inside. The original bagels were much thinner and lighter and they were not eaten as fresh because of the fact that they were baked off-site and they were sold, let's say, on the streets, so they had a harder denser crust. While I wouldn't say stale, I would say they didn't have the softness of the fresh bagel of today.

At some point there is a little bit of a division; the pretzel goes on and it lives its life and it becomes a sexy stadium product in the United States separate from the bagel we know. In the 16th century there exist some Jewish writings about the bagel, some references, for the first time to:

- when is it appropriate to eat a bagel?,
- discussion of bagels as a gift for newborn babies,
- as a discussion as a "bagel for the bris",
- as a discussion of "bagels for the Shiva Call",

All these things that are very tied into Jewish identity. This is part-and-parcel of the fact that in Germany, and then in Poland, the people who were involved in the baking were largely Jews. These Jews were, to some degree, as has been the history of Jews throughout modern history, relegated to only certain professions, relegated to only certain areas to live and they became the bakers.

Now, they were baking for Gentiles, for the most part, in many of the places where they were not even allowed to eat baked product-their own baked bread. This is, to some degree, where the notion that the bagel is boiled comes from because there was some odd dispensation that Jews could eat the boiled bread but they could not eat the baked bread. While this is a little bit strange, near the end of the 16th century, we start to see an increased level of discussion and writings about bagels. You then start to see Polish immigrants coming to this area (The Lower East Side of NYC). They physically relocate to this area and they start to establish Jewish communities, very ultra-orthodox communities. These were communities where Jewish people were aggregating and, as a result, to some degree, we come to view the Lower East Side as being the kickoff point for the United States bagel explosion.

Now, in terms of the preparation of the bagel, let us tie a lot of these things up in relationship to Jewish religious and dietary law. For those of you that understand that the bagel ties in nicely to Jewish culture and Jewish tradition from a religious standpoint because of the observation of the Sabbath. So, what occurs for those who are Sabbath observers come Friday at sundown? From that time on, basically, nothing goes on- we pray, we do little as it relates to social and to work. Especially in a society that is more homogeneous, like the Lower East Side was, the Sabbath is observed strictly and then at the break of the Sabbath there is a somewhat celebratory atmosphere. It is tradition to break fast and we eat. So the bagel, in its preparation, became an ideal product for these purposes. The bagel is rolled before Sabbath. It is a simple product, it is made of flour, it is made of yeast, it is made of water, it is made of salt. We do everything that we can for the preparation of the bagel before Friday at sundown and wait. And wait, until when? Until Saturday when the Sabbath is over! Now as a result of the waiting, there's a beautiful by-product of this; maybe it wasn't even the intended by-product, but what is the by-product? The by-product is that the bagel starts to gain flavor because it sits and the yeast works and, all of a sudden, the bagel gets a little puffier. The bagel's yeast starts to work. We start to get that sugar breakdown and all of a sudden you end up in a situation where you get a product that is, after 18 hours, ready to go. Now, the Sabbath ends, all you have to do is boil that bagel, bake it, and it is ready to go. So, it is an ideal product for Sabbath observation. This is a huge reason the bagel is identified with Jewish life.

So, those things really do tie-in hand-in-hand, while they may not have necessarily been all intended, it is, absolutely, part and parcel of what occurred. So, now when we have more bakers that move to the Lower East Side and they start to open more bakeries, there is a little bit of a change from the products and bagels of Eastern Europe. That change comes in two ways. The first was the flour used in the United States is a little different from the flour used in Europe. It was a little bit less whole-wheat based and it is a little bit less dense and it is a little higher in gluten. So, when I discussed earlier that the bagel in Europe was a little bit closer to the pretzel, even without changing the formula, when you came to the Lower East Side, the natural fact was that the bagel dough wasn't as dense and then when the gluten is working, the bagel gets a little bit puffier than its ancestors.

It's an important change, because historically, we are going to talk a little bit about cream cheese and lox; people didn't eat cream cheese and lox, Jews of the time did not eat cream cheese and lox, because there was no cream cheese and lox. There is no lox in Poland. No salmon in Poland, and there was certainly no cream cheese in Poland. What they had was chicken fat. They dipped a bagel in chicken fat. Sometimes a lardish type butter. So, we think about today the way people buy and eat bagels and you say, if I were to say to my kids on a Saturday morning: *"let's get some chicken fat and bagels"*, they would look at me like I was crazy. However, when the bagel came to the United States, because it was now a little bit puffier, because the hole was a little bit more closed, and it was a little bit softer, it became more ideal for what we'll talk about a little bit later on, which is the making of sandwiches. We will also see the fact that the bagel became more associated with high-class living to some degree and not ghetto living so, people weren't dipping product in chicken fat but, they were eating cream cheese, which was an elegant thing for people to eat.

The Jewish bakers had a stronghold in NYC, in terms of bakeries. In 1890 there were about 50 Jewish bakeries in this area. By 1900, there were almost double of that amount. The came to be tons of Jewish bakeries and a lot of Jewish people living in this area. It is a little bit hard for people to conceptualize as you walk through the gentrified Lower East Side, with today's beautiful buildings, a little bit different. This was a ghetto and people sold bagels on the street- many times on sticks, they were sold on sticks. They were baked in underground basements here complete with roaches, rats, and mice. Then they would take the bagels and put them on sticks and sell them on the street. So, what occurred on the Lower East Side was that the Jewish bakers got together and formed the Union and that Union became a very strong and powerful element in New York City. In fact, one of the things that is not always well-known is the impact of the Jewish unionization of the bakeries that led to almost an epidemic for employers throughout the city. The garment workers unionized and in other places bigger unions formed; much of that came from the unionization of the Lower East Side first.

Certain rules came into place, came into effect, some of what we will talk about later. One of the things that came into effect in those union rules were that all bagels needed to be made by hand. We will see how that comes into play later on, but a lot of it had to do with the conditions in which people were working, the conditions in which people lived in terms of trying to increase the standards with which you had a Local 338, which I should have mentioned, was the biggest bakery union.

Now, one of the biggest forces which is still around today, perhaps not as big a force as the unions but still a force, is the magazine or the newspaper "**The Forward**". **The Jewish Forward** for those of you who are familiar- they were very involved in doing something that was a little different, which was raising the consciousness of regular New Yorkers. What they would ask people in their scathingeditorials: *"Are you eating the food from the Jewish bakeries?"*. On a social level the bakers were in terrible conditions, maybe New Yorkers cared, maybe they didn't. *"You are eating stuff that's not made in sanitary conditions"*. This people cared more about that than the workers' conditions. That focus had the impact of increasing the cleanliness and the sanitation and all of those conditions for Jewish bakers who we working hard. If you think about the type of weather we had over the last couple days, 115 degrees on Sunday, think about being in 1900 in a basement in the Lower East Side making bagels.[2] It's really hard to fathom.

I talked a little bit about the chicken fat; I am gonna going to go into that, because there is an evolution of the sides and the lox and the cream cheese spreads as it relates to the bagel's popularity. You start to see an expansion of the bagel and the expansion of the popularity of the bagel, but still to a large degree only in Jewish circles and Jewish related circles. As New Yorkers' standard of living starts to

---

[2] During the week of this lecture in the Summer of 2019 NYC had experienced a record heat wave, over 100 degrees for several days in a row.

go up, you start to see the rise of something called *"the Kosher Style Deli"* largely in the Broadway area outside of the Lower East Side. *"The Kosher Style Deli"* starts to have sandwiches that are pastrami sandwiches, corned beef sandwiches, and bagel sandwiches.[3] So, the bagel starts to make its migration out of the Lower East Side and becomes exposed to wealthier people who are now going to see Broadway shows and might spend as much on a pastrami sandwich as they spent on the Broadway show and dinner; the pastrami sandwich was that expensive! So now, those people are eating bagels.

Fish had been always a part of the Jewish culture and tradition, Herring more so and Chubs[4] but, we start to see innovations in salting and things of that nature to preserve the product and it starts to become a delicacy that gets eaten with bagels. Simultaneously, cream cheese comes out of, believe it or not, not Philadelphia but Monroe, Chester New York. The invention of cream cheese was to duplicate some fancy cheeses that people were eating in Europe and it is so fancy that

---

[3] Many of these Delis have adopted Jewish Cuisine without the strict dietary Kosher laws being enforced.

[4] Chubs are generally small, whole whitefish.

the high-end restaurants in New York are serving cream cheese bricks as dessert, *"I'm done with dinner I'll have a brick of cream cheese"*; that becomes my dessert.

So, the Breakstone brothers, believe it or not, we know these names from food, the Breakstone Brothers say: *"we want to do a couple of things and one is we want to be able to make cream cheese more a part of the everyday diet"* and they start to come up with different ways to constitute it, so it's easier to spread.

They begin advertising in magazines and newspapers and places, trade papers, where Jewish people will be coming up with recipes for Hamantashen, and for different types of things, and it becomes a bagel spread.[5] So now, with *"The Kosher Style Deli"*, with the advent of lox and cream cheese, you get these great new sandwiches in the Broadway Kosher Style Delis. These become what

---

[5] A hamantash is a filled-pocket cookie or pastry recognizable for its triangular shape, usually associated with the Jewish holiday of Purim

we love today, what we call the Davidovich[6] here (at the Blue Moon Hotel Bagel Shop), which is the bagels lox and cream cheese, and which has become a staple of Jewish identity and Jewish cultural identity here, but not in Europe. It is not that you are going to go to Poland to look into the history of the bagel and say *"let me have it a Davidovich"*, unless they are trying to replicate a New York style.

You start to have this expansion but, you also start to have a change in the Jewish identity in New York. You have what people are calling, no longer so much religious Jews but Cultural Jews. They become called "Bagels and Lox Jews". They are also called the "Bagel Jews"; they are people who like their bagels, they love being Jewish, and they identify with (now as we are getting closer to post-World War II) Israel. They identify with Judaism, they observe the High Holy Days, but they may not be as inclined to keep strict Kosher. They may not be as inclined to be only living in Orthodox circles. You get now into a situation where the bagel is still relatively unknown and

---

[6] This is a traditional sandwich made with a water boiled Davidovich bagel, Sliced lox, plain Cream Cheese, capers and sliced onions.

in fact, there was a union strike in the 1950s and the **New York Times** wrote about it, because they called it *"the great bagel famine"* and the **New York Times'** sensibility was that people didn't know what a bagel was. So, **The New York Times**, this educated erudite paper, described the bagel *"as a unsweetened doughnut"*. That was **The New York Times'** definition of a bagel, *"and with a slight setting of more rigor mortis having set it"*, that's how **The New York Times** describes the bagel to people who, all throughout this area, still didn't know what a bagel was.

As more people are starting to understand what the bagel is and you start to see in various small places, the discussion of bagels, the terminology of bagels, you start to see something very interesting happens. We don't have Instagram, we didn't have Facebook, we don't have Twitter but, we still had social icons. So, in James Dean's short-lived career, this cool guy, *"rebel without a cause"*, is interviewed for **McCall Magazine**, at the time in huge distribution, and what does he say? *"I love bagels"*. Bagels? What are bagels?

James Dean likes bagels; it must be cool to eat bagels. Now the Gentiles are excited, *"we want eat bagels, like James Dean"*. So, all of a sudden, you start to see, and you can see how the world is different, but, the world is the same. I mean, now this is a totally different time.

Now we start to see the Borscht Belt comedians: Milton Berle, Jackie Mason, guys like that. Those guys are what are doing their circuit, they are around, they are introducing Jewish comedy to people and what do they call those circuits? They call this "The Bagel Circuit". *"I'm on the Bagel Circuit"*, which means basically at that time the Catskills and places of that nature. So, again, we are introducing as popular culture, as technology, as television, all of those things we have the expansion of the bagel.

Then a guy comes along, love him/hate him, angel/devil, a guy who forever changes the face of bagels in the world, it is actually Harry Lender. It's four people really. Harry Lender, his sons, Murray and Marvin Lender, and a guy by the name of Daniel Thompson.

Daniel Thompson was a West Coast inventor. He had invented the very exciting fold up Ping-Pong table. So now, you didn't have to have the Ping-Pong table taking up the whole basement, you could fold it and put it in the corner; that was Daniel Thompson's invention. But, he also invented something known as the bagel forming machine. The bagel forming machine would be what would help to modernize, from an efficiency standpoint, the bagel making process. It would eliminate people hand rolling the bagels, but it did something that is considered perfidy and really frowned upon to authentic bagel makers, which is this: the machine couldn't take the true bagel dough. The bagel dough was too thick. So, in order to use Daniel Thompson's machine, in order to be able to save the money that you needed to save on the labor, you needed to change the consistency of the bagel and make the bagel softer, make the bagel thinner, make the bagel more bread-like, more kaiser roll like, but as an economic trade-off. That itself, probably wouldn't have gone anywhere but, for the fact that the Lenders, out of New Haven Connecticut, little bagel makers, decided that they were going to culturize and make the Jewish identity of the bagel into a national identity. While they were not good bakers, they were not good at the bagel, but they were marketing geniuses. They funded Daniel Thompson so he could build his bagel machine and they came up with several new components of bagel business:

- #1- They came up with the idea, a very simple idea, to freeze bagels and ship them so that you no longer necessarily had to buy the bagels hot on the street. In those days, you couldn't walk into the supermarket and get your frozen bag of bagels, it didn't exist, and it was the advent of Murray Lender and Marvin Lender's concept that it did that.

- #2- They began using Daniel Thompson's bagel machine for production.

- #3- They began marketing the bagel just wildly and in any capacity. They ended up with television deals, for those of you who may remember, for me as a child, there was a program called *"Wonderama"*. Wonderama was a children's program, when you had limited amount of television shows. When you watch that show, if you go back and watch an old clip of it, all the children are wearing a necklace which is a bagel and a string, it's called *"a bagelette"*. That was a Lender. He partnered with Wonderama so that every little kid that walked into that show got a bagel necklace as a giveaway and that's part of his content.

- 4- The other thing that they did was they tried to look at how they could appeal to Gentiles. How they could appeal to non-Jews and get them to understand the product. So, they did something which, again, changed bagel making forever, but for bagel purists may be something that's upsetting. They said: *"let's look at the German breads, let's look at the Austrian breads, what are they familiar with?"* They (American Gentiles) are familiar with cinnamon, they're familiar with raisins in their bread so, we'll put that with the bagel and we'll make the cinnamon raisin bagel"*. So, actually Murray and Marvin Lender are responsible for this, the advent of the cinnamon raisin bagel, and the door opens to all of the different flavors of bagels that you have today.

They did a phenomenal job of doing a couple of things, of popularizing bagels and of putting a lot of people out of work. What happened is that they broke the back of the unions because the unions would only support people that made bagels by hand. Bakery owners could spend a little money invested on a machine, but become more profitable as a result of having to be able to pour out these bagels. This had a dramatic impact on it on the face of bagel making in the United States. And the interesting thing is that what surveys would start to show is that when discussing the Lender's bagel, almost across the board, people said: *"we think this is a garbage product but we buy it. Why? Because we can't get bagels where we are, out in the Midwest and the convenience. I don't have to go to some local store, they were pre-sliced. I can just take the Lender's bagel and put it in the oven. So, while I think it's a poor substitute, it's all I got."* So, it was a dramatic change in terms of the modernization of the bagel and the expansion of the bagel and it led to, and I made some notes when I was thinking about this, today we have the Green bagel, the Jalapeno bagel, the

Chocolate Chip bagel, and, again, the purists will cry about it, but it has helped sales.[7]

So, back to my original point about the expansion of the bagel- it's hard to imagine that in the world today, particularly, in the United States, whether you are Jewish or not, that you don't know the bagel is. You may not necessarily have all that much knowledge of the history of the bagel, or what it symbolizes but it has expanded greatly beyond the borders of Poland and the Lower East Side to the entire New York area, metropolitan area, and the entire country. Everybody knows what a bagel is, everybody has some concept. Now, many people think of it as the "*bread with the hole in it*", and that is partially true, but only partially true.

In order to really be, from my perspective, considered a bagel, a true bagel, first of all you have got to be boiled, it is the boiling that creates the shine. It's what creates the crust; it's what creates a density

---

[7] It is not uncommon to have 18-20 flavors of bagels for sale in a store even though sales of over 80% are in 5 flavors or less.

on the outside and doughiness on the inside. The products has got to sit for 18 hours, (12 to 18 hours), before it's boiled and baked. This process goes against modern efficiency; this is why so much of the bagel products today, are not like this, but like this (pointing to the Kaiser Roll).

It's not necessarily the dough that they use, that may be part of it, but you can sort of work around that. The issue is, that for a bagel to be a "real" bagel, you can't simply roll it, boil it and bake it. It kills the texture of it, it kills the taste of it. What happens today is, modern bagel makers change that formula to get it in the machine, they then roll it with chemicals, and then what they will do is the chemicals are supposed to speed up the process. They take the bagel, put it in an oven NOW. They don't want to take time to boil it, they steam it, and they turn around and serve it. So now you have a product that no longer has the same kind of dough, is no longer boiled; is no longer aged, so those products for the most part when you break them, when you taste them are like this (holds the roll again).

Now listening to different people talk, traditional bagels, they say: *"should be so chewy you feel it in your jaw"*. I am not sure necessarily everybody likes that, but I understand what they're talking about and again we think about the pretzel mentality. So what's the good news? The good news is that today, because of companies like **Davidovich**[8], sincerely, you can get good bagels anywhere in the country, it doesn't have to be Lender's because, for us what we do is we take your New York-Style bagel in one of our warehouses and we freeze it at about 90%. So, it's already got all the processes, the good ingredients, it sits for 18 hours, it is boiled, it is partially baked and then it is frozen. It then goes out to a store, let's say in California, where all they have to do is bake it off. Once they bake it off in in their facility, it's truly in New York-Style bagel because everything's been done in NYC except for the final baking of it.

---

[8] Davidovich is a NYC wholesale brand still making bagels using traditional Artisan practices.

There's a little bit of a discussion. I laugh when I hear it and that is the question of whether New York the only place that you can get really good bagels and the answer is: I haven't found anybody outside of New York, despite anything that they may say, that has managed to, across the board, consistently do bagels as well as New Yorkers can do bagels. Do I believe it? Now again, can you match up scientifically the water? Can you match up the conditions? Can you match up the ingredients? The answer is yes. Our history has been and, feedback has been, that there's just a difference between dough products, pizza as well, that you make in New York and ones that are made in other parts. The water is different, the air is different, everything about it is different, as well as the formula, as well as the ingredients. So, from our perspective, that's why we've had success in sending this product to Tennessee where, you might say: *"well, this product is made and frozen and shipped and re-baked and somebody makes the bagel from hand there"*, it's not necessarily going to have the same quality and the same and the same texture.

It's my belief, and I'm talking to David Page, from **David Page Productions**, he's the guy who produced *"Diners Drive-ins and Dives"*[9], about this concept and I think we've gotten to a point where, despite what we may talk about in terms of differences of bagels, the bagel has really gone from being a Jewish, European, Orthodox religious product, to an American product.

The most recent sort of reason for that to some degree, believe it or not, is the economic real estate bust of ten years ago. Now, why do I say that? The reason I say that is, we probably all know New Yorkers, who in a sort of Diaspora, left New York for better economic conditions when the real estate and the great recession took place. Those people took with them everything, including their appetite for New York food. They went to beautiful places in North Carolina and Las Vegas and places in Florida, where it may be very cheap to live, but you can't get yourself a good pastrami sandwich or a good bagels, lox, and cream cheese, and those people have to, in some degree,

---

[9] *Diners Drive-ins and Dives* is the highly successful Show starring Guy Fieri.

created a rebirth of interest in the same concept that was created by Murray Lender, which is the exporting of the New York bagel to local places. However, it's benefited because the fact of the matter is, since those people now have a lot less money to spend on New York taxes and on New York real estate problems, they are willing to spend a few extra pennies to get something better than the Lender's bagel.

So, for me, I appreciate you guys taking the time to talk about it, it's a subject of great interest, we could talk about any of these products and any of these ancillary products. I will also tell you, it just by the interesting note is, that while Lenders changed the face of it as it related to flavors, and while any bagel store you walk into in New York you might see 20 or 24 flavors, I'll tell you, I don't know any bagel place that probably sells more than five flavors as 50 to 80% of their sales. It is still Plain, it still Everything, it's still going to be Whole-Wheat, it's going be Onion, it's going be Garlic. It is still going be Pumpernickel, of course, if you're eating fish. So, you can come up with your Froot Loops and Marshmallow bagel all you want and there may be, somebody who has an appetite for it. Is it a bagel? Isn't it a bagel? I'm probably not the right guy to ask. However, at this point it hasn't changed the overall complexion of bagel sales. The only place, believe it or not, that we've seen a difference in the complexion is the Far East. We deal in the Far East and because there's a Blueberry craze there, they love blueberry bagels, but they have no historical relationship to the product for the most part. People didn't eat those kinds of breakfast foods, prior to 20 years ago, in China, in Korea, in Taiwan and now that they do, they're looking for something. But aside from that, this (Plain) is going to be for the most part your number one or number two seller, this and Everything bagel is probably 55% of anybody's bagel sales. I would venture to say, probably even Lender's so, on that note I'm more than happy to answer any questions that I can but, I think that sort of in time, it wraps it up.

The Questions

Audience Member Asks A Question About The Original H&H Bagels

So, I've worked with H&H[10] for a long time and, that's a very good it's an excellent example. Sure, the question was about the H&H story, what's the real of my relationship to H&H in the H&H story. So, H&H was a terrific example of what helped to make bagels from a New York food to a national food. The **Seinfeld** show is, really what really put H&H on the map. H&H was a great beloved, purveyor of bagels. They made bagels on the Upper West Side. They made bagels the old-fashioned way for a long time, and they did a lot of sending frozen par-baked bagels to other parts of the country. However, Jerry Seinfeld, New York boy, Jewish lover of bagels, Jerry Seinfeld is noted for saying: *"I would rather have a Barney Greengrass bagel than a bottle of Johnnie Walker",* if you were to give him a gift he would rather a Barney Greengrass bagel than a bottle of Johnnie Walker Blue. He did a famous episode about the strike at H&H, a famous union labor strike that took place at H&H, and it did so much to excite people about the brand.

---

[10] The speaker was a former employee of the Original H&H Bagels before it went out of business and wrote a tell all book about his experiences there in 2015.

I got involved with H&H at a time that, very sadly, the company had a significant amount, and this is all public record, a significant amount of tax debt, had a significant amount of problems, the stories in my book sort of read like fiction because, it ranged everything from bankruptcy to labor disputes, to murder, to criminal, to tax fraud, to all sorts of exciting things and what was at that point the most identifiable bagel company in the world and brand, ceased to exist. It was taken over by the government, they attempted to liquidate and essentially the brand died.

The positive thing that it tells you that's very interesting is, that when you have a strong brand, and they had a strong brand, is that 10 years later for the most part, people still know the name H&H and they still understand the name H&H, they still know what it is. The fact that Seinfeld is probably shown every single night somewhere in the world in reruns probably doesn't hurt that fact but, it just goes to show you, it's also the delicate balance between having a good brand and not settling and resting on those laurels, because having the good brand will make you indelibly identified in people's minds, but it won't keep the bagels rolling once the government comes in and shuts you down. So, you got to have a balance between all of those things, but it was an exciting time that I was there, it was exciting to see people. The last day that I was at H&H and they were closing, people were legitimately heartfelt, crying on the Upper West Side and the reason is, because not so much that they knew they couldn't get bagels, because they knew they could get bagels, it was because it represented for them. As I said at the beginning of the talk, a time in their life when Mom and Dad took them teething to H&H Bagels, and they were teething on a bagel instead of a teething ring, and it brought for them very emotional stories and emotional connections to their family, to their culture, to their city and to their childhood and that's one of the reasons why being in the bagel business is fun, because there's an identity to it. There's never a time that I speak to somebody that they don't, that they can't tell you about some relationship between the bagel and their life and their family.

Question About Whether Any Companies Still Use Artisan Bagel Practices

Sure, it's a great question. So, for the most part your local bagel stores still make bagels the old-fashioned way. For the most part what I'm talking about is going to be your supermarket or your chain bagel stores or your bagels that are made by big wholesalers. Most of them do not use Artisan practices.

People send me these crazy things, so they sent me a bag of big bagels and it had King Kong on the Empire State Building holding a bagel saying "New York City Bagels", "New York Style bagels", and when you look closely at the print you see it was made in Hong Kong and they had all the right things, because they understand that New York is the King of bagels.

Question About Kosher Status of Bagels

Yes, we make all of our bagels in a facility that is Kosher, and then we ship them out and were shipping for our source. The process is Artisan and the Bagels are Artisan and Kosher. In fact, if you go online, you can see some of the videos of the kettle boiling, just exactly the same equipment that was historically used, including the rotating all-fired, deck ovens, people rolling by hand, seeding by hand and again. One of the traits is that the bagels are Kosher and Kosher Certified. One of the things to understand quickly, in the interest of time is that, when the stuff was in Europe, you didn't have kosher certification, you just had kosher. But, when you came to the United States, there's a whole dynamic of different types of food so, the products that were being made the same way and although they were kosher we needed to be able to demonstrate that they hadn't deviated from Kosher practices,: *"we need to have kosher certification to insure that they're doing it the old-fashioned way"*. So Kosher Certification began to emerge but that is a whole different lecture. Our bagels are, also, and it's something that's important, especially because it's tied into Jewish identity. Our bagels are kosher, they're high Kosher, they're certified by the OK and they're Pas Yisroel, which again, is that our ovens are essentially ignited by Rabbis and that light stays on, and if that light goes out, you essentially have to call the rabbi to come and light the oven.

Thank you for coming and I thank you for your interest in learning about the Real History of Bagels in America.

Made in the USA
Monee, IL
26 May 2023

34708585R00025